A Bouquet of Flowers

Compiled By Anna Nicholas

Paul Cézanne (1838-1906) *Flowers in a Delft Vase*

Grange
BOOKS

Karen Armitage *Polyanthus at Hurst*

A Bouquet of Flowers

Compiled By Anna Nicholas

Pierre Auguste Renoir (1841-1919) *Flowers in a Vase*

A selection of poems and quotations

Acknowledgments

The Publishers would like to acknowledge the following
for permission to reproduce copyright material:
Pages 19 and 21, Adrian Henri and Jonathan Cape
Limited for 'Honeysuckle' and 'Garden, Giverny'; Page
22, Society of Authors and Jonathan Cape Limited for
'Loveliest of Trees, the Cherry Now' by A.E.
Houseman; Pages 26, 31, and 39, Jonathan Cape
Limited and the Hogarth Press for 'Heartsease', 'The
Chrysanthemum Show' and 'Stephanotis' by C. Day
Lewis from *The Poems of C. Day Lewis*; Pages 40, 42,
and 43, Faber & Faber for 'They Told Me', 'The
Bindweed' and 'The Sunken Garden' by Walter de la
Mare from *The Collected Poems of Walter de la Mare*.

The Publisher has made every effort to trace copyrights
holders of material reproduced within this
compilation. If, however, they have inadvertently made
any error they would be grateful for notification.

Many thanks to Paperchase, London for kindly allowing
us to use their papers.

Pictures courtesy of Bridgeman Art Library

Published in 1994 by Grange Books
An imprint of Grange Books PLC
The Grange, Grange Yard
London SE1 3AG

ISBN 1 85627 626 0

Printed in Italy

Jan Van Kessel (1626-1679) *Butterflies and Other Insects*

Could you understand
One who was wild as if he found a mine
Of golden guineas, when he noticed first
The soft green streaks in a Snowdrop's inner leaves?

Robert Buchanan 1841-1901

George Frederick Watts (1817-1904) *Cheerful Spring from my Window*

J. Worsley (20th century) *Primroses, Violets and Other Flowers*

eight

Though storms may break the Primrose on its stalk,
Though frosts may blight the freshness of its bloom,
Yet Spring's awakening breath will woo the earth
To feed with kindliest dews its favourite flower,
That blooms in mossy banks and darksome glens,
Lighting the greenwood with its sunny smile;
Fear not then, Spirit, Death's disrobing hand.

Percy Bysshe Shelley 1792-1822

From: Hamlet

A violet in the youth of primy nature,

Forward, not permanent, sweet, not lasting,

The perfume and suppliance of a minute;

No more.

William Shakespeare 1564-1616

Sir James Dromgole Linton (1840-1916) *Violets*

Walter de la Mare 1873-1956

Beatrice Parsons (1870-1955) July Flowers, Oaklands, Rugeley

De la Mare suffered a severe illness and for some time his life lay in the balance. During his convalescence, his daughter came to see him and asked if there was anything she could get him – fruit or flowers. 'No, no,' said the poet weakly, 'too late for fruit, too soon for flowers.'

eleven

I love its growth at large and free
　　By untrod path and unlopped tree,
　　　Or nodding by the unpruned hedge,
Or on the water's dangerous edge
Where flags and meadowsweet blow rank
With rushes on the quaking bank.

On a Bed of Forget-Me-Nots by Christina Rossetti 1830-1894

Helen Bradley (1900-1979) *Dusk in the Enchanted Garden*

twelve

Beatrice Parsons (1870-1955) *Spring Woods, Gravetye, Sussex*

Fair daffodils, we weep to see
You haste away so soon;
As yet the early-rising sun
Has not attained his noon.
Stay, stay,
Until the hasting day
Has run
But to the evensong;
And, having prayed together, we
Will go with you along.
We have short time to stay, as you,
We have as short a spring;
As quick a growth to meet decay,
As you, or anything.
We die,
As your hours do, and dry
Away,
Like to the summer's rain;
Or as the pearls of morning's dew
Ne'er to be found again.

Robert Herrick 1591-1674

thirteen

Alfred Sisley (1839-1899) Bouquet de Fleurs

Paul Meurisse, French actor 1912-1979

Meurisse, renowned for his taciturnity, once caught sight of a sign in a florist's window: 'SAY IT WITH FLOWERS.' He went in and asked for a rose. 'Just one,' he told the young clerk. 'To be delivered to this address with my card.' The girl picked out a delicate red rose and asked, 'Is there any message?' Meurisse took the flower and plucked out all the petals except two. 'There you are,' he said handing back the mutilated bloom. 'And even then, I wonder if I haven't said too much.'

fourteen

Ralph Todd (fl. 1800-1893) *Young Girl with a Hoe outside a Cottage*

David Woodlock (1842-1929) *A Cottage Door*

From: Much Ado About Nothing

And bid her steal into the pleached bower,

Where honeysuckle, ripen'd by the sun,

Forbid the the sun to enter, like favourites,

Made proud by princes

William Shakespeare

Alfred Sisley (1839-1899) *Misty Morning*

seventeen

Dante Gabriel Rossetti (1828-1882) *La Ghirlandata*

For fourteen years he loved her from
four door away. After seven years
she planted honeysuckle at her door.
Often, returning drunk,
its smell would turn the night to poetry.
Her image at the back of his mind,
persistent as a rhymescheme. One year
she gave him honeysuckle soap
for Christmas. Her husband asked him round
for drinks. After the honeysuckle,
two children, who grew as quickly.
Soon her family will move away,
scented vines abandoned. Tonight,
she lies in his arms, palpable as syllables,
soft as nightsmelling flowers, promises herself
within four years. Outside her bright blue door
unattended tendrils wither in the first frost.

Adrian Henri

Edward Kington Brice (b. 1860)
Lilies, Delphiniums and Poppies in the Garden of the Artist's Cottage at Ashton-under-Hill

George Bernard Shaw 1856-1950

Arnold Bennett visited Shaw in his apartment and, knowing his host's love of flowers, was surprised that there was not a single vase of flowers to be seen. He remarked on their absence to Shaw: 'But I thought you were so fond of flowers.' 'I am,' said Shaw, 'and I'm very fond of children too, but I don't chop off their heads and stand them in pots about the house.'

twenty

Delphiniums, sweet williams,
purple gladioli,
against yellow asters, marigolds,
the whirls of sunflowers;
glimpsed pink walls against emerald shutters.
A bamboo-grove
lurks in the shadows by the lily-pond,
patient as a tiger.
Lovers kiss on a Japanese bridge
watched by the bearded phantom
from behind the willows,
sad as a blind girl in a summer garden.

Garden, Giverny by Adrian Henri

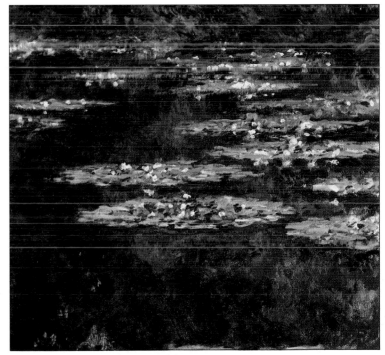

Claude Monet (1840-1926) *Waterlilies*

Loveliest of trees, the cherry now
Is hung with bloom along the bough,
And stands about the woodland ride
Wearing white for Eastertide.
Now, of my threescore years and ten,
Twenty will not come again,
And take from seventy springs a score,
It only leaves me fifty more.
And since to look at things in bloom
Fifty springs are little room,
About the woodlands I will go
To see the cherry hung with snow.

A.E. Housman 1859-1936

Beatrice Parsons (1870-1955) *White Summer*

twenty-three

William Stephen Coleman (1829-1904) *Cottage Garden in Summer*

Welcome, maids of honour!
You do bring
In the spring,
And wait upon her.
She has virgins many,
Fresh and fair;
Yet you are
More sweet than any.
You're the maiden posies,
And so graced
To be placed
'Fore damask roses.
Yet, though thus respected,
By-and-by
Ye do lie,
Poor girls, neglected.

To Violets by Robert Herrick 1591-1674

M.V. Morgan (fl. 1880-1930) *Snowdrops and Violets*

Helen Allingham (1848-1926) *The Orchard in the Spring*

Do you remember that hour

In a nook of the flowing uplands

When you found for me, at the cornfield's edge,

A golden and purple flower?

Heartsease, you said. I thought it might be

A token that love meant well by you and me.

I shall not find it again

With you no more to guide me.

I could not bear to find it now

With anyone else beside me.

And the heartsease is far less rare

Than what it is named for, what I can feel nowhere.

Once again it is summer:

Wildflowers beflag the lane

That takes me away from our golden uplands,

Heart-wrung and alone.

The best I can look for, by vale or hill,

A herb they tell me is common enough – self-heal.

C. Day Lewis 1925-1972

Arthur Claude Cooke (b.1867) *Spring in the Orchard*

Beatrice Parsons (1870-1955) *The Sundial, Brook House, Sussex*

twenty-seven

Ask me why I send you here
This sweet Infanta of the year?
Ask me why I send to you
This primrose, thus bepearl'd with dew?
I will whisper to your ears:-
The sweets of love are mix'd with tears.
Ask me why this flower does show
So yellow-green, and sickly too?
Ask me why the stalk is weak
And bending (yet it doth not break)?
I will answer:- These discover
What fainting hopes are in a lover.

Robert Herrick 1591-1674

Myles Birket Foster (1825-1899) *At the Cottage Door*

Shut not so soon; the dull-eyed night
Has not as yet begun
To make a seizure on the light,
Or to seal up the sun.
No marigolds yet closed are,
No shadows great appear;
Nor doth the early shepherd's star
Shine like a spangle here.
Stay but till my Julia close
Her life-begetting eye,
And let the whole world then dispose
Itself to live or die.

Robert Herrick

Beatrice Parsons (1870-1955) *Foxgloves and Daisies*

Music, when soft voices die,
Vibrates in the memory;
Odours, when sweet violets sicken,
Live within the sense they quicken.
Rose leaves, when the rose is dead,
Are heap'd for the beloved's bed;
And so thy thoughts, when thou art gone,
Love itself shall slumber on.

Percy Bysshe Shelley

George Samuel Elgood (1851-1943) *Summer Flowers, Ramscliffe*

Here's Abbey Way: here are the rooms
Where they held the chrysanthemum show –
Leaves like talons of greenfire, blooms
of a barbarous frenzy, red, flame, bronze –
And a schoolboy walked in the furnace once,
Thirty years ago.
You might have thought, had you seen him that day
Mooching from stall to stall,
It was wasted on him – the prize array
Of flowers with their resinous, caustic tang,
Their colours that royally boomed and rang
Like gongs in the pitchpine hall.
Any tongue could scorch him; even hope tease
As if it dissembled a leer:
Like smouldering fuse, anxieties
Blindwormed his breast. How should one feel,
Consuming in youth's slow ordeal,
What flashes from flower to flower?
Yet something did touch him then, at the quick,
Like a premature memory prising
Through flesh. Those blooms with the bonfire reek
And the flaming of ruby, copper, gold –
There boyhood's sun foretold, retold
A full gamut of setting and rising.
Something touched him. Always the scene
Was to haunt his memory –
Not haunt – come alive there, as if what had been
But a flowery idea took flesh in the womb
Of his solitude, rayed out a rare, real bloom.
I know, for I was he.
And today, when I see chrysanthemums,
I half envy that boy
For whom they spoke as muffled drums
Darkly messaging, 'All decays;
But youth's brief agony can blaze
Into a posthumous joy.'

C. Day Lewis 1925-1972

Claude Monet (1840-1926) *Chrysanthemums*

Just then, beneath some orange trees,
Whose fruit and blossoms in the breeze
Were wantoning together, free,
Like age at play with infancy...

Thomas Moore (1779-1852)

Albert Cox (fl.1900) *Walled Garden in Statuary*

Henry Sutton Palmer (1854-1933) *The Cottar's Pride – a Cottage Garden*

By all those token flowers that tell

What words can never speak so well.

Lord Byron

Odilon Redon (1840-1916) *Poppies and other Flowers in a Vase*

Beatrice Parsons (1870-1955) *Columbine*

The rose is the perfume of the Gods,
The joy of men,
It adorns the blossoming charms of Love,
It is Venus's dearest flower.

Henri Fantin Latour (1836-1904) *Narcisses Blancs, Jacinthes et Tulipes*

A Garden is a lovesome thing,

God wot!

Rose plot,

Fringed pool

Fern'd grot –

The veriest school

Of peace: and yet the fool

Contends that God is not –

Not God! in gardens!

When the eve is cool?

Nay, but I have a sign;

'Tis very sure God walks in mine.

Thomas Edward Brown 1830-1897

David Woodlock (1842-1929) *A Welsh Homestead*

The red rose whispers of passion,

And the white rose breathes of love;

O, the red rose is a falcon,

And the white rose is a dove.

But I send you a cream-white rosebud

With a flush on its petal tips;

For the love that is purest and sweetest

Has a kiss of desire on the lips.

John Boyle O'Reilly 1844-1890

Albert Williams *White Roses in a Glass Vase*

Timothy Easton *Herb Garden at Noon*

Pouring an essence of stephanotis

Into his bath till the panelled, carpeted room

Breathed like a paradise fit for sweltering houris,

He lapsed through scent and steam

To another bathroom, shires and years away —

A makeshift one tacked on to

The end of a cottage, it smelt of rusting pipes,

Damp plaster. In that lean-to

One night she sprinkled the stephanotis

He'd given her — a few drops of delicate living

Tasted by two still young enough to need

No luxury but their loving.

They are long parted, and their essence gone.

Yet even now he can smell,

Infused with the paradise scent, that breath of rusty

Water and sweating wall.

C. Day Lewis 1925-1972

They told me Pan was dead, but I
Oft marvelled who it was that sang
Down the green valleys languidly
Where the grey elder-thickets hang.
Sometimes I thought it was a bird
My soul had charged with sorcery;
Sometimes it seemed my own heart heard
Inland the sorrow of the sea.
But even where the primrose sets
the seal of her pale loveliness,
I found amid the violets
Tears of an antique bitterness.

Walter de la Mare 1873-1956

Ernest Albert Chadwick (1876-1955) Madonna Lilies

Say it with flowers.

Slogan for Society of American Florists

Walter Crane (1845-1915) *Madonna Lilies in a Garden*

Albert Moore (1841-1893) Forget-Me-Nots

The bindweed roots pierce down
  Deeper than men do lie,
Laid in their dark-shut graves
Their slumbering kinsmen by.
Yet what frail thin-spun flowers
She casts into the air,
To breathe the sunshine, and
To leave her fragrance there.
But when the sweet moon comes,
Showering her silver down,
Half-wreathed in faint sleep,
They droop where they have blown.
So all the grass is set,
Beneath her trembling ray,
With buds that have been flowers,
Brimmed with reflected day.

Walter de la Mare 1873-1956

Speak not – whisper not;
Here bloweth thyme and bergamot;
Softly on the evening hour,
Secret herbs their spices shower.
Dark-spiked rosemary and myrrh,
Lean-stalked purple lavender;
Hides within her bosom, too,
All her sorrows, bitter rue.
Breathe not – trespass not;
Of this green and darkling spot,
Latticed from the moon's beams,
Perchance a distant dreamer dreams;
Perchance upon its darkening hour,
The unseen ghosts of children fare,
Faintly swinging, sway and sweep,
Like lovely sea-flowers in the deep;
While, unmoved, to watch and ward,
Amid its gloomed and daisied sward,
Stands with bowed and dewy head
That one little leaden Lad.

Walter de la Mare 1873-1956

forty-three

Come into the garden, Maud,
For the black bat, Night, has flown,
Come into the garden, Maud,
I am here at the gate alone;
And the woodbine spices are wafted abroad,
And the musk of the roses blown.

For a breeze of morning moves,
And the planet of Love is on high,
Beginning to faint in the light that she loves
On a bed of daffodil sky,
To faint in the light of the sun she loves,
To faint in his light, and to die.

All night have the roses heard
The flute, violin, bassoon;
All night has the casement jessamine stirr'd
To the dancers dancing in tune;
Till a silence fell with the waking bird,
And a hush with the setting moon.

I said to the lily, 'There is but one
With whom she has heart to be gay,
When will the dancers leave her alone?
She is weary of dance and play.'
Now half to the setting moon are gone,
And half to the rising day;
Low on the sand and loud on the stone
The last wheel echoes away.

I said to the rose, 'The brief night goes
In babble and revel and wine.
O young lord-lover, what sighs are those
For one that will never be thine?
But mine, but mine,' so I sware to the rose,
'For ever and ever, mine.'

Alfred Lord Tennyson 1809-1892

Claude Strachan (b.1865-c.1929) *At Dunster*

Charles Edwin Flower (b. 1871) *King's Manor Garden at East Hendred*

Mary, Mary, quite contrary,
How does your garden grow?
With silver bells and cockle shells,
And pretty maids all in a row.

Tommy Thumb's Pretty Song Book, c. 1744

When this winter rose
Blossoms amid the snows,
A symbol of God's promise, care and love.

Anon

Jan Brueghel (1568-1625) *A Basket of Flowers*

Lavender is for lovers true,
Which evermore be fain,
Desiring always for to have
Some pleasure for their pain.

Elizabethan Lyric